# ROBOTS AND ROBOTICS
# Robots at Work and Play

# Tony Hyland

Smart Apple Media

This edition first published in 2008 in the United States of America by Smart Apple Media.

Smart Apple Media
2140 Howard Drive West
North Mankato, Minnesota 56003

First published in 2007 by
MACMILLAN EDUCATION AUSTRALIA PTY LTD
627 Chapel Street, South Yarra, Australia 3141

Visit our Web site at www.macmillan.com.au or go directly to www.macmillanlibrary.com.au

Associated companies and representatives throughout the world.

Library of Congress Cataloging-in-Publication Data

Hyland, Tony.
    Robots at work and play / by Tony Hyland.
    p. cm. — (Robots and robotics)
    Includes index.
    ISBN 978-1-59920-117-7
    1.  Robots, Industrial—Juvenile literature. 2.  Mechanical toys—Juvenile literature.  I. Title.

    TJ211.2.H545 2007
    629.8'92—dc22

                                                                    2007004663

Edited by Margaret Maher
Text and cover design by Ivan Finnegan, iF Design
Page layout by Ivan Finnegan, iF Design
Photo research by Legend Images

Printed in U.S.

**Acknowledgements**
The author and the publisher are grateful to the following for permission to reproduce copyright material:

Front cover photograph: Wakamaru robot from Mitsubishi © Issei Kato/Reuters/Picture Media.

Photos courtesy of:
© Peter Arnold, Inc./Alamy, p. 11; © Sally and Richard Greenhill/Alamy, p. 24; © FANUC Robotics, pp. 9, 13, 14; Koichi Kamoshida/Getty Images, p. 20; Douglas McFadd/Getty Images, p. 16; © Hasbro, p. 18; John Deere, p. 15; ©2006 The LEGO Group, pp. 5, 22, 23; Photolibrary/© Leslie Garland Picture Library/Alamy, p. 12; Photolibrary/Maximilian Stock Ltd/Science Photo Library, pp. 7, 8, 10; Photolibrary/David Parker/600-Group/ Science Photo Library, p. 4; Photolibrary/© Jeremy Sutton-Hibbert/Alamy, p. 19; © Reuters/Picture Media, p. 28; © Issei Kato/Reuters/Picture Media, pp. 1, 17; © Kimberly White/Reuters/Picture Media, p. 29; © The RoboCup Federation, pp. 26, 27; © Science Museum/Science & Society Picture Library, p. 6; Valiant Technologies/www.valiant-technology.com, p. 25; Wow Wee Ltd, p. 21.

Background textures courtesy of Photodisc.

# Contents

**GLOSSARY WORDS**

When a word is printed in **bold**, you can look up its meaning in the glossary on page 31.

# Robots

There are more and more robots in the world. Once they were just figments of the imagination, metal creatures that clanked through old **science fiction** movies and books. Robots today are real, and you will find them in the most surprising places. Some are tiny, no bigger than a fly. Others are among the largest machines on Earth.

Robots are machines that can move and think for themselves. Most robots work in factories, doing endless, repeated tasks faster than any human. Other robots explore places that humans cannot safely reach. Some robots go to the bottom of the sea. Others go to the rocky surface of Mars.

There are also **surgical robots**, robots that carry out scientific experiments, and robots that **disarm** bombs. Today's toys often include robot technology—you can even **program** your own toy robot.

Where do robots fit into your life?

Most robots work in factories.

# Robots at work

In factories around the world, robots work on a huge range of jobs. There are giant machines that stamp metal sheets into car parts or load coal in a mine. These jobs are often called the three Ds—dirty, dull, and dangerous. Other robots are smaller and gentler, packing delicate items without crushing them. These robots work almost every hour of the day. They stop only for essential cleaning and repairs.

# Robots at play

Some robots are made just for fun. There are simple toy robots that can be programmed with a few buttons, or kit robots to build. People can make robots that can walk, dance, or even play soccer. You can even build your own battle robot. Armed with hammers, drills, and saws, these giants battle each other in weekly TV contests. Victory goes to the best and smartest robot, not always the strongest.

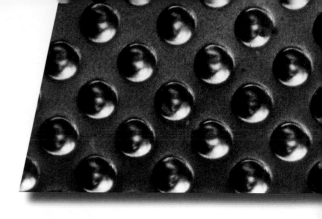

Some robots are great fun to play with.

5

# Industrial robots

The very first real **industrial** robot was a one-armed robot called Unimate. It was built in 1961 and was used for stacking hot metal parts. It could lift up to 2 tons at a time. Unimate's program was stored on a metal drum inside the robot, not on a computer.

After Unimate, more robots started to appear in factories. Today, there are over 150,000 robots in factories around the world. They do many kinds of jobs, from packing food to **welding** car parts together. Humans could do these jobs, but robots can work faster and are less expensive.

Unimate was the very first industrial robot.

## ROBOFACT

### WHICH COUNTRY HAS THE MOST ROBOTS?

There are more robots in Japanese factories than in all of the rest of the world put together. They work at everything from assembling cars to preparing food.

# Programming robots

Robots cannot do anything without a program. This is a long and complex set of instructions. It is planned and stored on a computer.

## Using a virtual model

Often, the program is developed using a **virtual model** of the robot. The model moves through the steps of its task. As it does this, the movements are automatically stored in the program. If there are any mistakes in the program, the computer model will not work correctly. The programmer keeps improving the program until it is exactly right. Then, the program can be loaded into the real robot.

## Teaching a robot

Part of programming an industrial robot is walking the machine through its steps. A worker holds the robot's arm and pushes it in the correct path. The robot stores this basic pattern of movements in its **memory**. Then the programmer makes any small changes needed using a computer.

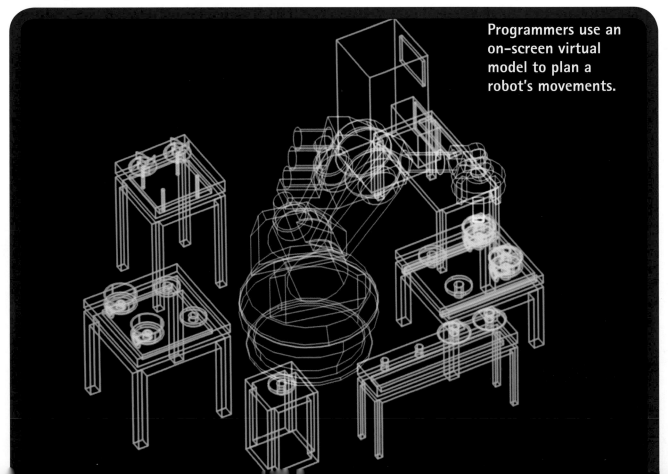

Programmers use an on-screen virtual model to plan a robot's movements.

# Robots in the car industry

Most of the world's industrial robots work in car factories. Each robot does one specific job on the car **assembly line**.

## Car assembly

Robots are good at doing the simple, repeated tasks involved in putting cars together. They are very fast and accurate. Some common jobs for robots are:

※ Stamping metal. The robot picks up flat sheets of metal and places them on a **press**. The press stamps the metal into the shape of a car part, such as a roof or a door panel. Then the robot removes the part and stacks it.

※ Welding. The robot welds metal parts together.

※ Assembly. The robot joins parts by bolting them together.

## ROBOFACT

### CAN ROBOTS DO EVERY JOB?

Many jobs are too complicated for robots. Humans work on jobs such as assembling engines, installing seats and fittings, and setting up electrical wiring. These jobs need human skill and judgment.

Each robot on an assembly line does a small part of the whole job.

# Spray painting

Once the car body has been assembled, it travels along the assembly line to the factory's painting section. Here, the car is spray painted.

## Why do robots make good painters?

Spraying paint is an ideal job for robots. The chemicals used in the paint can be harmful to humans. Robots can spray the correct amount of paint, in a perfect pattern, for every car. Human painters occasionally make mistakes. They might spray too much paint or leave uneven marks.

## Robots on rails

Robot spray painters are not always fixed to the floor like other industrial robots. They often travel on a rail beside the assembly line. Sometimes they hang above it on a moving platform. This lets the robot move along with the car, spraying as it goes. The arm twists up, down, and around, spraying into every hidden corner of the car body.

Robots can spray paint accurately all over a car body.

# Robotic packing machines

Packing robots collect newly made items and pack them into containers. This is a job that humans could do, but it is very boring and repetitive.

## Packing and palletizing

Packing robots are used in many industries. Some stack large, heavy machinery. Others pack food or drinks into cartons. Palletizers stack goods onto wooden platforms called **pallets**. Forklifts carry the loaded pallets to waiting trucks.

Packing robots work very quickly, repeating the same movements over and over. They use a vision system to detect the items they are packing. They must apply just the right amount of force to pick up the items. If they squeeze too hard, they can crush the items. If they don't squeeze hard enough, the items will slip.

# ROBOFACT

## A SPEEDY PACKER

The world's fastest packing robot can pack 3,000 items per hour. That's 50 items every minute. It can lift and pack loads of up to 90 pounds.

Robotic packing machines are fast and efficient.

# Boxed chocolates

Fancy, boxed chocolates are difficult to pack, even for humans. They can be easily squashed or broken. Robots designed to pack chocolates need to be very fast but gentle.

## Sorting the shapes

In the past, chocolate companies always employed humans to pack their boxed chocolates. Today, most chocolate factories use food-packing robots. Food-packing robots use a **three-dimensional visual system**. This helps them see the different shapes that go into chocolate boxes. As the chocolates pass along the assembly line, the robot scans the shapes. It picks up the one it needs and places it into the correct spot in a box.

## Gentle grippers

Food-packing robots are different from conventional robots. They have special gentle grippers to hold food without damaging it. Often these are fitted with vacuum tips. The robots must also be very clean. The grippers are changed and sterilized regularly to prevent passing bacteria to the food.

Robots can pack chocolates into gift boxes quickly and carefully.

# Danger—stay clear!

Industrial robots are huge, heavy machines. It is dangerous for humans to be near them when they are working. Robots can easily swing around and crush any human.

## Out of harm's way

Industrial robots only have enough sensors to let them do their job. They have no way to detect that a person is near them. They do not even know what a human is.

For this reason, industrial robots normally work inside a cage called a **cell**. Human controllers watch the robot from outside the cell. Sometimes the workers need to check the robot's equipment or change the **end effectors**. They switch off the robot's power before they enter the cell.

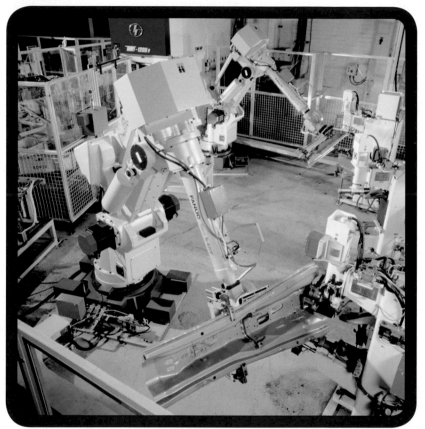

Workers stay outside the safety cell when a robot is switched on.

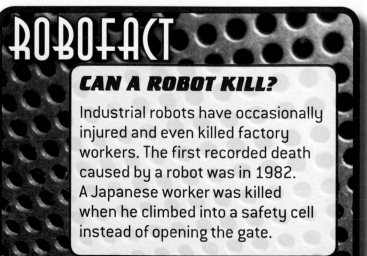

## ROBOFACT

### CAN A ROBOT KILL?

Industrial robots have occasionally injured and even killed factory workers. The first recorded death caused by a robot was in 1982. A Japanese worker was killed when he climbed into a safety cell instead of opening the gate.

# Up Close

**ROBOT**
M-900iA

**JOB**
Industrial robot

**MAKER**
FANUC Limited, Japan

**SKILLS**
Heavy lifting, spot welding, spray painting

**SIZE**
10 feet (3 m) tall

**WEIGHT**
6,200 pounds (2,800 kg)

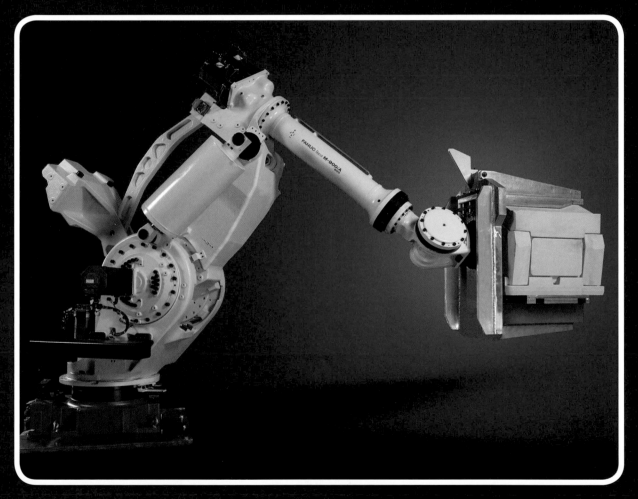

The M-900iA is the largest robot made by FANUC Limited. It is a huge robotic arm, used in many large car factories around the world. The M-900iA can lift car parts weighing up to 1,300 pounds (590 kg). It has six separate joints, so it can move in any direction.

The robot can weld thousands of spots on a car body without stopping. Its movements are extremely fast and accurate. It uses a three-dimensional laser sensor to "see" where it is working. The spots that it welds are never more than 0.1 inches (3 millimeters) out of line.

# The spread of robots

The earliest industrial robots mainly worked in the car industry. Today, robots can be found in almost any type of factory.

## Precision cutting and sanding

Robotic arms make very precise movements. Robots fitted with saws cut and shape the wooden parts of guitars. Other robots sand and smooth the pieces. Robots fitted with cutters, grinders, and polishers make parts for many other items, from toys to fighter jets.

## Assembling parts

Robotic arms can put together small parts for engines, gearboxes, and even toys. The robot reaches into bins of parts. It selects the correct pieces and quickly builds the entire item. **Touch sensors** allow the robot to press and tighten parts to just the correct pressure.

Smaller industrial robots can cut and shape material precisely.

# ROBOFACT

### SIZE MATTERS

Robotic arms are not all huge machines. Small assembly robots would fit easily on a tabletop, and weigh only a few pounds. They are useful for making small items such as disk drives.

14

# *Moving out of factories*

Robots these days do not all work in factories. Once researchers developed ways to make robots more mobile, they could work in many other places. Most robots working outside factories are on wheels or tracks. Some move around on legs.

## Improving robot vision

Most industrial robots do not have **vision sensors**. They rely on touch sensors to work out their position. However, robots that move around must be able to work out exactly where they are. They use a combination of vision sensors and other sensors such as **sonar** and **infrared sensors**.

## Improving robot intelligence

Early industrial robots had very limited intelligence. They could be programmed to do one simple task. Modern industrial robots can be programmed to handle complicated tasks, such as assembling engines. Improved intelligence makes it possible for mobile robots to move around in our world. They can now do many different jobs safely.

The R-Gator robotic vehicle can drive cross-country, guided by vision sensors.

# Robots in the home

Science fiction stories sometimes show robots helping around the home, doing all the boring chores. However, so far it has been too difficult to make real robots that work like this. In our homes, the most common robots are toys, not workers.

## Floor cleaners

The most common working robots in homes are small floor-cleaning robots, which vacuum or polish. They roll along randomly, changing direction whenever they meet a wall or other obstacle. Owners can set up a **virtual wall**. This is an **infrared light** that stops the robot from wandering off into another room.

## Power supply

Robotic cleaners run on rechargeable batteries. When their power is running low, they automatically go to their recharging station.

### ROBOFACT

**WHY DON'T VACUUM ROBOTS FALL DOWN STAIRS?**

Floor-cleaning robots use infrared sensors to detect changes in the floor. When they come to stairs, the robots automatically stop and turn in another direction.

Robots that move from place to place have sensors to stop them bumping into things.

# *Robots that work with people*

Even though some home robots are designed to work with people, they do not recognize human beings. They simply roll along, doing their job. It will be many years before robots actually communicate with us.

## A domestic care robot

The Japanese Wakamaru is the first working model of a **domestic robot**. It is a **humanoid** robot, designed to provide company for the elderly or disabled. It recognizes up to 10 faces, and understands 10,000 words.

Wakamaru can't do any real work such as cleaning. It performs services, such as recording messages and appointments. It provides company for sick or elderly people.

## What would a domestic robot be like?

A true domestic robot would need to recognize the people in the family. It would also need to be simple to operate.

Domestic robots will probably not look humanoid. They are more likely to look like a washing machine on wheels, with several arms and hands.

The Wakamaru robot can help take care of elderly people.

17

# Toy robots

Toy robots come in many shapes and sizes. Some are very simple models, but others work almost like real robots.

## Toy robots over the years

The earliest toy robots were produced in the 1930s. They were very simple by today's standards. Today, there are many different kinds of toy robots. The simplest ones are plastic models, such as Transformers and Mobile Suit Gundam robots. These can be folded and changed into several different shapes. More complex toy robots, such as Robosapien, can be programmed to perform a series of actions.

Some of today's dolls and teddy bears use robot technology. They smile and frown, laugh and cry, and react to their owner's voice. These abilities are controlled by built-in robotic microchips.

## ROBOFACT

### ROBOTS ON TV

Many robot toys are based on TV series, such as *Transformers* or *Eureka 7*. The toys look exciting, but they are models, rather than programmable robots.

Toy robots can be plastic models or programmable robots.

# Up Close

**ROBOT**
Aibo

**JOB**
Programmable robot dog

**MAKER**
Sony Corporation, Japan

**SKILLS**
Walking, dancing, responding to owner's voice commands

**SIZE**
10 inches (25 cm) long

Aibo is a toy robot, made to look and act like a dog. When it is first started, Aibo acts like an inquisitive puppy. It will walk around, exploring the area. When its batteries run low, Aibo seeks out its battery charging unit. It "sleeps" while the batteries are recharging.

Like a puppy, Aibo learns to recognize the voice and face of its owner. It stores this information as part of its program, and gradually learns to obey more voice commands. Aibo appears to enjoy playing with its owner. It looks sad when there is no one to play with.

Aibo can also be programmed to perform more complex tasks. Aibo can dance in time to music, and even play soccer.

# Transformers

Transformers are among the most popular robot toys today. Several sets of the toys have come out since they were first released in 1984. Each set has a different style and appearance. The Transformers figures start as large plastic robots. With a few twists and turns of their cleverly designed bodies, each Transformer can be changed into a completely different toy. Most of the Transformers change into cars, trucks, or planes. The Beast Wars Transformer characters transform into wild animals such as cheetahs and rhinos.

# Mobile Suit Gundam

The popular *Mobile Suit Gundam* TV series features characters similar to the Transformers. Human characters pilot the huge robotic Gundam suits. These suits can transform into terrifying battle robots. Gundam toys come in several different sizes. Each is able to transform into a fighting vehicle.

Mobile Suit Gundam toy robots can transform into different shapes.

# Up Close

**ROBOT**
Robosapien V2

**JOB**
Programmable robot

**MAKER**
Wow Wee Limited, Canada

**SKILLS**
Seeing, hearing, talking

**SIZE**
24 inches (61 cm) tall

Robosapien looks like an ice hockey player, with huge shoulder pads and a helmet-like head. It can walk or run around. It is controlled by a built-in computer program.

The robot comes with a wireless remote control. Owners can push buttons to raise and lower the robot's arms and legs and turn it in different directions.

Robosapien is programmable. The owner can enter a whole program of commands into the robot's memory at once. Pushing the correct button makes the robot go through the whole program. It can even dance in time to music.

Robosapien has a set of touch sensors and sound sensors. These allow the robot to react to bumping into something, or to hearing certain sounds. It can pick up items from the ground and throw them.

# Robot kits

You can make your own robot, using one of the many kits available. Robot kits include parts to make the body of the robot. They also have computer chips to store the robot's program.

## Building your robot

Companies such as Lego have made construction kits for many years. Owners can put together pieces to make many different models.

Now the same pieces come with robotic technology. The model can be programmed to perform a set of actions. Small motors drive the wheels, or make legs and arms move.

## Programming your robot

Real robots are controlled by complicated programs. However, toy robot kits use much simpler programs. Commands such as FORWARD 10 and LEFT 90 will make the robot go forward and then turn left.

Users program Lego Mindstorms robots with a series of command icons.

## ROBOFACT

### USING THE NET

Whatever kit you use, you will find information on the Internet about it. You can find the latest information before it gets into books or magazines.

# Lego Mindstorms kits

Lego Technics consist of gears, wheels, and other pieces that can be made into simple machines. Lego has combined these pieces with a computer built into a large plastic block. This mix of new and older technology is called Mindstorms.

The Mindstorms kits allow users to design and build their own robots. Users can then program the robots using an ordinary computer. The programs are sent from the computer to the block using an infrared light.

## Adding sensors

New sensors have been developed to go with the Mindstorms kits. Robots can be fitted with light sensors, which allow them to follow or avoid light. Microphones and touch sensors allow the robots to react to sound and touch.

The newest series of Mindstorms is known as NXT. It allows users to build and program robots such as the Scorpion and the Bulldozer.

Lego Mindstorms NXT, assembled into a Scorpion robot.

# Robots at school

Robots at school can help students learn about math and science. Many schools take part in robotics competitions, such as Robocup. This helps students learn how robots really work.

## Robots for young students

Young students can learn using robots such as the Roamer. This simple robot has motorized wheels and a set of buttons with numbers and symbols. Students can press a sequence of buttons and watch as the robot follows the program.

## Robots for older students

Older children often use kits such as Lego Mindstorms. Students can program their robots to do simple things, such as following a line. Later, they learn to program more complex behavior, such as playing soccer or dancing.

## ROBOFACT

### WHY LEARN ABOUT ROBOTS?

By the time today's elementary school children grow up, robots will be much more common. It is important to learn what robots can do, and how to control them.

Young children can learn to control the Roamer robot.

# Seymour's turtle

Seymour Papert is a South African teacher who helped bring robots into schools. During the 1960s, he developed ideas for using robots with schoolchildren.

## Before there were robots

In the 1960s, there was no such thing as a workable small robot. Papert developed the idea of using a turtle robot to help children learn basic mathematical ideas.

The turtle could move around on a sheet of paper. It held a pen which drew basic shapes as it moved. Papert had also developed a simple computer programming language, called Logo. Students could use Logo to tell the turtle to move forward and backward and to turn around.

## Turtles and other robots

Today, there are turtle-shaped robots that can do what Seymour wanted. There are also other simple robots, such as the Mindstorms robots, which Seymour helped develop. Seymour Papert's dream has come true, and children really can learn to use robots in classrooms.

Students can control the turtle robot by using the Logo programming language.

# Robocup

Every year, thousands of students enter robots in a soccer competition known as Robocup. This competition was originally only for robotics students at the college or university level. Now, students of all ages can join in.

## Why play soccer?

Programming robots to play soccer is good practice for programming robots in industry. The robots must move around on a playing area, find the ball, and push it toward their goal. At the same time, the other team is trying to get the ball.

## Controlling the robots

The robots are not radio-controlled. Once the game starts, the robot teams must figure out their own strategy for getting the ball and defeating their opponents. They rely on clever programming by the students.

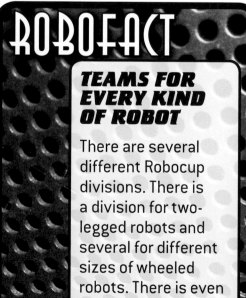

## ROBOFACT

### TEAMS FOR EVERY KIND OF ROBOT

There are several different Robocup divisions. There is a division for two-legged robots and several for different sizes of wheeled robots. There is even a four-legged division for Aibo robots.

Two-legged robots play in the Robocup Soccer competition.

School students can enter robots in the Robocup Junior competition.

# *Robocup Junior*

The Robocup Junior competition is open to elementary and high school students. Most of the robots are made from Lego Mindstorms parts. However, teams can make robots from other materials if they wish.

## Playing soccer

The main Robocup Junior competition is soccer. The game is played by teams of four robots on a flat playing field. One robot rolls from side to side in front of the goal, keeping the ball out. The other three robots try to push or kick the ball toward their goal. Because the robots have limited built-in vision, the ball sends out infrared signals. This helps the robots detect where it is.

## Other Robocup competitions

Besides soccer, there is a rescue competition. Robots have to follow a marked trail to "rescue" a small chocolate figure. There is also a dance competition, where robots dance in time to music.

# Battlebots

The most spectacular robot competitions are the Battling Robots, or Battlebots. There are several different leagues, but the idea is always the same—smash the other robot!

## TV spectacle

Battlebots appear on TV. They battle in pairs, like boxers. The object of the competition is to beat the other robot in any way possible. Some robots are armed with saws or drills to rip and cut at their opponent. Others use strong claws or flippers to lift the other battlebots and flip them over.

## Almost a robot

Although the battlebots use robot technology, strictly speaking they are not robots. The machines are radio-controlled by their owners. Battlebots do not yet have the level of artificial intelligence to fight battles by themselves.

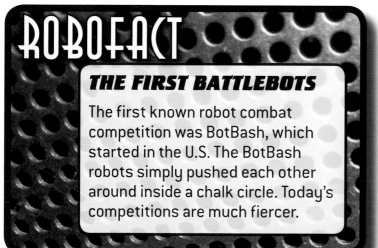

## ROBOFACT

### THE FIRST BATTLEBOTS

The first known robot combat competition was BotBash, which started in the U.S. The BotBash robots simply pushed each other around inside a chalk circle. Today's competitions are much fiercer.

BioHazard is a combat robot which has won the Battlebots World Championships several times.

# *Building a Battlebot*

Competitors can build Battlebots of almost any size. The largest robots weigh 390 pounds (177 kg), while the smallest are only about 1 pound (0.45 kg). Robots compete against other robots of the same weight.

## Designing the robot

Designers try to make Battlebots wide and low to the ground. This makes it harder to flip them over. Users also design strong armor that will resist the other team's weapons. They include batteries to drive the robot's motors, and a radio-control mechanism.

## Building the robot

Teams spend many hours building their robots. There are no kits for these robots—every robot is a special design. All parts are made by the team.

## Going into battle

In the competition, one controller handles the radio control. The other team members cheer and give advice to the controller. The events are often televised, and teams don't want to see their robot defeated on national television.

**Many Battlebots have powerful weapons to defeat their opponents.**

# Build a robot

You can build your own robot and program it. Your first efforts may be very simple, but as you learn more you can make robots that do complicated tricks. It is easiest to start with a kit robot.

## What you need

- A complete robot kit: Lego Mindstorms, Fischer-Technic, or any other kit.
- Instructions. You'll need to follow these exactly the first time you build your robot.
- A computer.

## What to do

1. Read the instruction booklet.
2. Follow the instructions carefully to build your robot.
3. Ask for help if you get stuck—friends and teachers may be able to help.
4. Program the robot using a computer.

Once the robot can do what it is supposed to do, start experimenting. What can you do to make your robot faster, stronger, or just better?

The job might be easier if it is a team effort. You will find that other students at your school are interested in helping. All of the Robocup Junior teams have several people involved, building and programming their robot.

Have fun!

# Glossary

**assembly line** - a conveyor belt in a factory where parts are added to gradually build an item

**cell** - a strong safety cage to keep humans away from working robots

**disarm** - to make an unexploded bomb safe

**domestic robot** - a robot that works in an ordinary home

**end effectors** - tools fitted to the end of a robotic arm

**humanoid** - similar in shape to a human

**industrial** - used in a factory

**infrared light** - light waves that are invisible to humans

**infrared sensors** - electronic devices that detect and measure levels of infrared light

**memory** - the part of a robot's computer that stores information

**pallets** - a plastic or wooden storage platform that can be lifted by a forklift

**press** - a machine for pressing flat steel sheets into car body parts

**program** - to install the instructions that control a robot's actions

**science fiction** - stories based on futuristic scientific ideas

**sonar** - a system that uses sound and echoes to detect objects

**surgical robots** - robots capable of performing surgical operations

**three-dimensional visual system** - a vision system with two cameras that allows a robot to see solid shapes accurately

**touch sensors** - electronic devices that detect and measure levels of pressure when touching something

**virtual model** - a three-dimensional model that appears on a computer screen

**virtual wall** - a beam of infrared light that a robot is programmed not to pass

**vision sensors** - electronic devices that detect light and objects visible to humans

**welding** - joining pieces of metal by heating the edges so they melt together

# Index